AMERICAN PRESIDENTS

WILLIAM J. CLINTON

INDIA JAMES

NorwoodHouse Press

Cataloging-in-Publication Data

Names: James, India.
Title: William J. Clinton / India James.
Description: Buffalo, NY : Norwood House Press, 2027. | Series: American presidents | Includes glossary and index.
Identifiers: ISBN 9781978580022 (pbk.) | ISBN 9781978580039 (library bound) | ISBN 9781978580046 (ebook)
Subjects: LCSH: Clinton, Bill, 1946---Juvenile literature. | Presidents--United States--Biography--Juvenile literature. | Legislators--United States--Biography--Juvenile literature.
Classification: LCC E886. J36 2027 | DDC 973.929092--dc23

Published in 2027 by
Norwood House Press
2544 Clinton Street
Buffalo, NY 14224

Designer: Rhea Magaro
Editor: Kim Thompson

Photo credits: Cover, p. 1 The White House; pp. 5, 8, 9, 11, 12, 16, 17, 19, 21 Wikipedia; p. 6 Nadia Yong/Shutterstock.com; p. 8 Winston Tan/Shutterstock.com; p. 10 Dennis MacDonald/Shutterstock.com; pp. 12-14 Library of Congress; p. 15 SRA William Rafter, USAF; p. 18 Joseph Sohm/Shutterstock.com; p. 20 lev radin/Shutterstock.com;

Printed in the United States of America

Some of the images in this book illustrate individuals who are models. The depictions do not imply actual situations or events.

CPSIA compliance information: Batch #CSNHP27: For further information contact Norwood House Press at 1-800-237-9932.

TABLE OF CONTENTS

Early Years

William Jefferson Clinton was born on August 19, 1946, in Hope, Arkansas. He grew up with his mother and stepfather. He has been known all his life by the nickname "Bill."

Birthplace in Hope, Arkansas

Bill took part in many activities while he was growing up. He was a Boy Scout. He played the saxophone. He sang in his church choir.

When he was in high school, Bill took a trip to visit the White House in Washington, D.C. He met the president. Bill decided he wanted to be president one day.

Building a Career

Bill went to college at Georgetown University in Washington, D.C. Then, he went to law school at Yale University.

Yale University

After he graduated, Bill married Hillary Rodham. They had one daughter, Chelsea.

Bill tried to become a member of the United States **House of Representatives**, but he lost the election. Later, he was elected **governor** of Arkansas. People liked him as a leader. They elected him to be governor a total of five times.

Presidency

In 1992, Bill was elected as the 42nd president of the United States. He was only 46 years old.

Presidents choose many advisers to help them do their job. Bill picked many women and **minorities** for these roles.

Bill focused on the country's money. He wanted to make sure that the nation did not spend more money than it had. This is called a balanced **budget**.

Bill helped the U.S. balance its budget. In fact, the country had a **surplus** of money while he was president.

It was important to Bill that the U.S. had good relations with other countries. He signed an agreement called the North American Free Trade Agreement (NAFTA). It made it easier for the U.S., Canada, and Mexico to buy and sell things from each other.

Bill was friendly and **outgoing**. He invited many different people to visit the White House. He played the saxophone to entertain them.

Later Life

Bill served two **terms** as president. After leaving the White House, Bill and Hillary moved to New York.

Bill helped his wife run in elections. She became a **senator** from New York. She ran for president in 2008 and 2016.

Bill started the Clinton Global Initiative. Its goal is to improve the lives of people all over the world.

Presidential Medal of Freedom, 2013

Bill Clinton continues to help his country. People remember him as a skilled and caring president.

Glossary

budget (BUHJ-it): a plan for how much money will be earned and spent over a period of time

governor (GUHV-ur-nur): the elected leader of a U.S. state

House of Representatives (house uhv rep-ri-ZEN-tuh-tivz): one of the two parts of the United States Congress that is made up of 435 members who help make laws for the country

minorities (muh-NOR-i-teez): groups of people of a particular race, ethnic group, or religion who are living among a larger group made up of people of a different race, ethnic group, or religion

outgoing (OUT-goh-ing): warm, friendly, and confident

senator (SEN-uh-tuhr): one of two people elected to represent a U.S. state in the Senate, which helps makes laws for the country

surplus (SUR-pluhs): an amount greater than what is used or needed

terms (turmz): definite or set periods of time; American presidents are elected to a term that lasts four years

Thinking Questions

1. What did Bill Clinton like to do as a child?
2. When did Bill decide he wanted to be president?
3. Who did Bill hire to help him as president?
4. What instrument does Bill play?
5. What does the Clinton Global Initiative do?

Index

About the Author

India James writes about science, technology, math, and history for young readers. She loves learning new things while writing books. India lives in Ohio with her family.